# What's it like to live in ...?

# France

by Jillian Powell

HODDER
*Wayland*

An imprint of Hodder Children's Books

# Other titles in the What's it like to live in? series:

# Canada    Italy    Jamaica

© 2003 White-Thomson Publishing Ltd

Produced for Hodder Wayland by
White-Thomson Publishing
2/3 St Andrew's Place, Lewes, East Sussex BN7 1UP

Published in Great Britain in 2003 by Hodder Wayland,
an imprint of Hodder Children's Books.

Editor: Kay Barnham
Designer: Tim Mayer
Consultant: Lorraine Harrison
Language consultant: Norah Granger – Former head teacher
and senior lecturer in Early Years Education at the
University of Brighton.
Picture research: Shelley Noronha – Glass Onion Pictures

The right of Jillian Powell to be identified as the author of
this Work has been asserted by her in accordance with the
Copyright, Designs and Patents Act 1988.

British Library Cataloguing in Publication Data
Powell, Jillian
   What's it like to live in France?
   1. France - Social life and customs - Juvenile literature
   2. France - Social conditions - Juvenile literature
   I. Title
   306'.0944
ISBN 0 7502 4295 7

Printed and bound in China

Hodder Children's Books
A division of Hodder Headline Limited
338 Euston Road, London NW1 3BH

**Picture acknowledgements**
Eye Ubiquitous (Selby) 20; HWPL (Dorian Shaw), 24;
James David Travel Photography 7, 15 & 28; Popperfoto
(Stefano Rellandini) 25; Rex Features Ltd (Bruno
Bebert/SIPA Press) 11; Robert Harding Picture Library 12,
(Tony Demin) 1 & 10, (Tony Gervis) 14, (C Martin) 13;
Sylvia Corday (Nick Rains) 23, (Geoffrey Taunton) 6, (J
Worker) 22; Topham Picturepoint cover, 27; Travel Ink
(David Martyn Hughes) 9, (Simon Reddy); WTPix (Chris
Fairclough) 28, 29. All other pictures HWPL.
Map artwork: The Map Studio.

Every effort has been made to trace copyright holders.
However, the publishers apologize for any unintentional
omissions and would be pleased in such cases to add an
acknowledgement in any future editions.

# Contents

# Where is France?

France is in western Europe. It is a large country bordered by the sea and by eight other European countries.

People enjoy sitting at outdoor cafés in towns and cities.

Over 60 million people live in France. Its capital is called Paris. France is famous for its varied countryside, fine cooking and delicious food.

4

France's place in the world

## FRANCE FACTS

France is the largest country in Europe.

The island of Corsica is part of France.

The largest cities are Paris, Marseille and Lyon.

France has over 3,000 kilometres of coastline.

UNITED KINGDOM

English Channel

BELGIUM

Lille

LUXEMBOURG

GERMANY

Seine

■ Paris

Brest

Rennes

Orléans

Loire

Dijon

Nantes

SWITZERLAND

F R A N C E

ATLANTIC OCEAN

Bay of Biscay

Massif Central

Lyon

Rhône

A l p s

ITALY

Bordeaux

N

W    E

S

Toulouse

Nice

MONACO

Marseille

P y r e n e e s

ANDORRA

Corsica

0    100 kilometres

0    100 miles

S P A I N

MEDITERRANEAN SEA

5

# Cities

Most people in France live in large towns or cities. Many of these cities began as ports or market places hundreds of years ago.

▼

Bordeaux is a beautiful city and port near the west coast of France.

The Eiffel Tower is a famous landmark in Paris. It is visited by six million people every year.

Today over two million people live in Paris. Another ten million live in the **suburbs**. Millions more come to visit Paris for its shops, museums and **art galleries**.

# The landscape

France has two high mountain **ranges** – the Pyrenees in the south and the Alps in the east. Mont Blanc, in the Alps, is the highest mountain in Europe.

During the summer months, goats graze in the Pyrenees.

8

Lavender is grown in the valleys of Provence in southern France.

The Massif Central is a large area of low mountains in the south. The rest of France is made up of **plains**, valleys and rolling hills.

# The weather

Mountain areas have warm summers, but the winters can be very cold, with heavy snow. The highest mountains are covered with snow all year round.

Snowboarding is a popular winter sport.

Beaches in the south of France have plenty of sunshine.

The south of France has **mild**, rainy winters and long, hot summers. The weather in the north is cooler and wetter, but summers are still warm.

# Transport

People travel around France by car, bus, train and plane. In towns, people often use scooters and motorbikes to get about.

France has some of the fastest trains in the world. They are called **TGV**s.

Ships and boats visit ports such as Marseille and Bordeaux. Paris and Lille have underground train **networks** so people can avoid the traffic above ground.

In France, people pay to use the motorways.

# Farming

A third of France's land is used for farming. In the north, there are beef and dairy farms. Farmers grow **cereal** crops too.

Dairy farmers keep cows for their milk. This is also made into butter and cheese.

In the drier south, farmers grow fruit and vegetables, such as olives. They also grow grapes for making wine. France is famous for its **champagne** and wine.

Sunshine ripens the grapes for harvest in the autumn.

15

# Food

France is famous for good food and cooking. Different areas have their own special dishes and foods. In Normandy, many recipes use apples and cream.

Flaky pastries called croissants are eaten at breakfast.

Family meals are an important part of the day. Many French families get together for meals at midday and in the evening.

This fish stew is made using a French recipe. It contains fish, shellfish and cream.

# Shopping

French people use lots of fresh fruit and vegetables in their cooking.

In France, many people like to shop for fresh foods every day. Some small shops sell just one sort of food, like bread or cakes.

18

France also has hypermarkets. These are very large supermarkets where people can buy everything from food and drink to clothes and household goods.

Hypermarkets are often built outside big towns and cities, where there is lots of room for them.

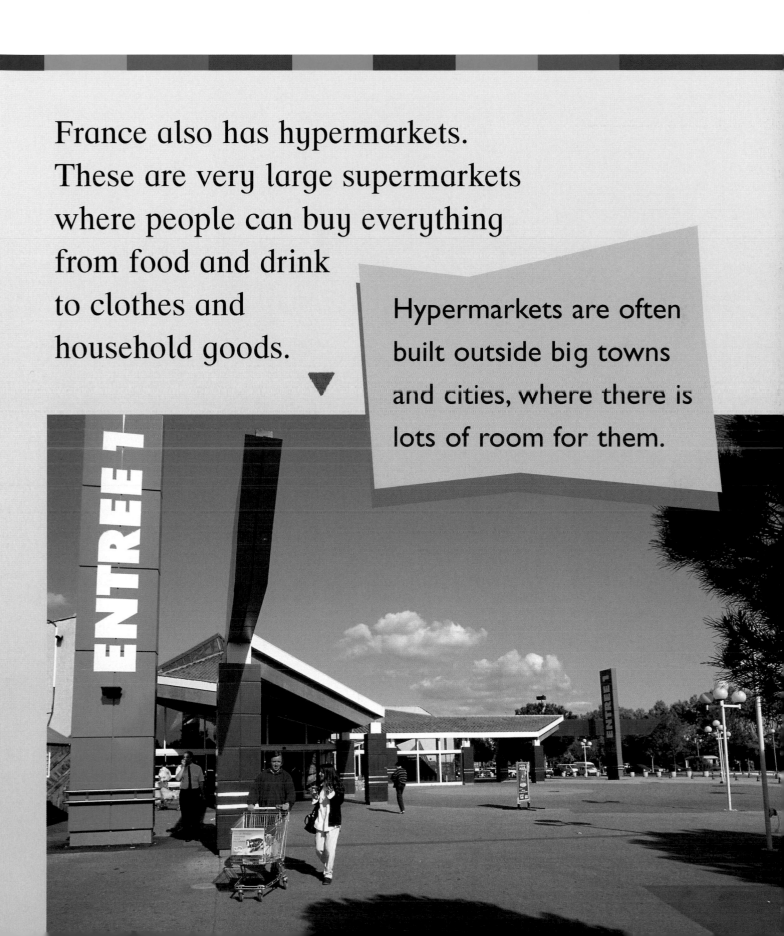

# Houses and homes

In French cities, many people live in blocks of flats. In smaller towns and villages, there are more houses and bungalows.

Balconies mean that people can use the space outside their flats.

These tall houses are hundreds of years old. They were built with brick and wood.

Many French houses and flats have shutters at the windows. The shutters can be closed to keep out the sun in summer and the cold in winter.

# At work

France has many different **industries**. Factories make machinery, aircraft, cars, chemicals, clothing and **textiles**. French goods, including cheeses and wines, are sold all over the world.

French cars are popular in France and other countries.

In the Alps and seaside areas, **tourism** is the main industry. Hotels and restaurants can be busy for many months of the year.

Many French people work in the tourist industry, looking after visitors to their country.

# Having fun

The most popular sports in France are football, tennis, basketball, rugby and judo. People who live near mountains do not have to travel far to snowboard and ski.

French people enjoy playing a game called 'boules'.

24

Many French people like to cycle. The Tour de France takes place every July. This is one of the toughest cycling races in the world.

During the Tour de France, cyclists cover thousands of kilometres.

# Festivals

Over four hundred **festivals** are held in France each year. Bastille Day on 14 July celebrates the day in 1789 when France became a **republic**.

On Bastille Day, fireworks light up the night sky in Paris.

The Mardi Gras Carnival parades through the streets of Nice every **Shrove Tuesday**.

As well as Christmas and Easter, there are many smaller festivals. Some are saints' days, others celebrate **regional produce** like wines and cheeses. There is even a snail festival.

27

# French scrapbook

This is a scrapbook of some everyday French things.

A card for taking part in a running competition at school.

This is a postcard of the Eiffel Tower in Paris.

The French use euro notes and coins. These can be spent in many countries in Europe.

A ticket to a
football match.

A bus
ticket.

A school
bus pass.

This boat ticket is used for
travel to île de Groix in
north-west France.

# Glossary

**Art galleries** Places where paintings, sculptures and other types of art are displayed.

**Cereal** A crop such as wheat, grown for food.

**Champagne** Fizzy wine made in the Champagne area of France.

**Festivals** Times of celebration.

**Industries** Work that employs lots of people, often in factories.

**Mild** A way of describing weather that is gentle rather than very hot, very cold or very wet.

**Networks** A system of railways or roads that link up with each other.

**Plains** Large areas of flat ground.

**Ranges** Rows of mountains or hills.

**Regional produce** A product that is made in a particular area.

**Republic** A country governed by a president.

**Shrove Tuesday** The day before Lent. Traditionally, Lent is a time of fasting for Christians.

**Suburbs** Areas on the edges of a city where people live.

**Textiles** Materials used for clothes and furnishings.

**TGV** This stands for *train à grande vitesse,* which means 'very fast train'.

**Tourism** Work to do with visitors and holidaymakers.

# Further information

## Some French words

| | |
|---|---|
| *au revoir* | bye, see you again |
| *bon appetit!* | enjoy your meal |
| *bonjour* | hello |
| *la boulangerie* | bread shop |
| *la carte postale* | postcard |
| *le déjeuner* | lunch |
| *le dîner* | dinner |
| *la fête* | festival |
| *la glace* | ice cream |
| *le musée* | museum |
| *la pâtisserie* | cake and pastry shop |
| *le petit déjeuner* | breakfast |
| *la poste* | post office |
| *merci* | thank you |
| *s'il vous plaît* | please |

## Books to read

A *Flavour of France* by Teresa Fisher (Hodder Wayland, 1998)

*Next Stop France* by Fred Martin (Heinemann Children's Library, 1998)

*Step Into France* by Clare Boast (Heinemann Children's Library, 1998)

*We Come From France* by Teresa Fisher (Hodder Wayland, 2001)

# Index